By: Sylvie Cyr

ARCHWAY PUBLISHING

Archway Publishing books may be ordered through booksellers or by contacting:

Archway Publishing
1663 Liberty Drive
Bloomington, IN 47403
www.archwaypublishing.com
1 (888) 242-5904

Because of the dynamic nature of the Internet, any web addresses or links contained in
this book may have changed since publication and may no longer be valid. The views
expressed in this work are solely those of the author and do not necessarily reflect the
views of the publisher, and the publisher hereby disclaims any responsibility for them.

Any people depicted in stock imagery provided by Thinkstock are models,
and such images are being used for illustrative purposes only.
Certain stock imagery © Thinkstock.

ISBN: 978-1-4808-5286-0 (sc)
ISBN: 978-1-4808-5287-7 (e)

Print information available on the last page.

Archway Publishing rev. date: 02/16/2018

Happy New Year!

cupid

Happy Easter

Happy Easter

Mother's Day

Mother

I love you Mom!

Father's Day

Feb. 12

Feb. 22

GEORGE AND
THE Cherrytree

1776

LIBERTY

JULY

4th

HOOOOOOOOO

Merry Christmas